The Tent

Lalie Harcourt & Ricki Wortzman

Illustrated by Mark Thurman

Dominie Press, Inc.

"Look what I got for my birthday," said Amy. "It's a new tent."

"Wow! Can we sleep in it tonight?" asked Gina.

"What a great idea," said Amy.

Gina looked in the box and said, "This will be easy to put together! Go ask your parents if we can have a sleepover in your backyard. I'll set up the tent."

3

Gina got to work. "I know exactly what to do," she said to herself. "I'm sure I've seen this tent on TV."

Gina took the long poles and made two triangles. She took two other poles and joined them to the top of the triangles.

4

When Amy returned, Gina and Amy put the canvas over the top pole.
"We're almost done," Gina said. "Get ready for our sleepover!"

Amy helped Gina out from under the canvas.
"Let's try again," Amy suggested. "I'm sure this
is like my uncle's tent. I know how to set it up."

The girls talked about their sleepover as they worked.

"There," said Amy, "we did it! Let's get our sleeping bags and our flashlights."

Amy looked in the box. "You'd think they'd put some instructions in here," she said.

"How hard can this be? It's a tent! It's a simple tent!" said Gina.

Amy and Gina stared at the different parts.

"I know!" said Gina. "Maybe it should be shaped like your house."

It was getting dark. Amy and Gina finally put the canvas around the poles. "We're finished!" said Amy. "Get ready for some scary stories and popcorn!"

14

"Enough already," said Amy. "Let's just sleep inside my house tonight!"

The girls got ready to go inside. They picked up the poles. Then they picked up the box.